Mortar & Pestle

Mortar & Pestle

Poems by Lisa Gill

New American Poetry Series

© 2006 by Lisa Gill
First Edition
Library of Congress Control Number: 2005932917
ISBN: 0-89823-231-7
New American Poetry Series
Cover design and interior book design by Brooke Kranzler
Author photograph by Bill Nevins

The publication of *Mortar & Pestle* is made possible by the generous support of the
McKnight Foundation and other contributors to New Rivers Press.

For academic permission please contact Frederick T. Courtright at 570-839-7477 or
permdude@eclipse.net. For all other permissions, contact The Copyright Clearance
Center at 978-750-8400 or info@copyright.com.

New Rivers Press is a nonprofit literary press associated with Minnesota State University
Moorhead.

Wayne Gudmundson, Director
Alan Davis, Senior Editor
Thom Tammaro, Poetry Editor
Donna Carlson, Managing Editor
      Editorial Assistant: Michelle Roers
      Graduate Assistant: Andria Tieman
      Mortar & Pestle book team: Michelle E. Peterson, Stephanie Schilling,
          Elizabeth Walkup
      Editorial Interns: Jeff Armstrong, Samuel Beaudoin, Greg Boose, Rebeca
          Dassinger, Crystal Gibbins, Joel Hagen, Michelle E. Peterson, Miranda
          Quast, Stephanie Schilling, Heather Steinmann, Jered Weber
      Design Interns: Melissa Davidson, Brenda Davis, Brooke Kranzler, Christopher
          Larson, SueAnn Lutkat, Dan Swenson, Lindsay Van Hoecke
      Festival Coordinator: Heather Steinmann
      Assistant Festival Coordinator: Miranda Quast
      Web Site Intern: Lindsey Young
Deb Hval, Business Manager
Allen Sheets, Design Manager
Liz Conmy, Marketing Manager

Printed in the United States of America.

New Rivers Press
c/o MSUM
1104 7th Avenue South
Moorhead, MN 56563

www.newriverspress.com

To Mitch and Mom and Mark
for supporting me through my first big flare.

Table of Contents

Preface

Lisa Gill began her career as a young poet by giving to her community. She organized the Herland monthly reading series for women writers and published *The Rag*, an ingenious one-page literary magazine. She was the instigator of The Poet's Diner, an inspired mix of poetry reading, dinner out, and fundraiser. She had the good sense to grow her poetry muscles while supporting the work of others, surrounding and immersing herself in the poetry scene, even as she helped create it. Living rural on the outskirts of town, supporting herself working construction until recent struggles with multiple sclerosis landed her on Social Security Disability, Lisa Gill is gutsy and visionary with both feet on the planet, an intellectual mud wrestler.

You probably think I am her best friend saying this, but I really only know her through her work and what I've heard about her works in the world of Albuquerque, a long, hot ninety miles from my home in La Puebla. By turning to the world of poetry as a contributor, a giver to community, she paid some mighty dues to the muses and they return the favor.

Whether it be tackling her hundred poems in *Red as a Lotus: Letters to a Dead Trappist* or a chapbook dealing with her diagnosis of MS, her work succeeds by dint of the Rilke dictum, "A work of art is good if it has grown out of necessity. In this manner of its origin lies its true estimate: there is no other" (*Letters to a Young Poet*). Her work blooms out of inner necessity and reaches the reader with mind-light, essential language, writing what can't be resisted, perhaps talking as much to clarify for herself as to the world.

Yet it is because Gill grounds her inner and personal in the external world that the work in *Mortar & Pestle* is so vivid. I think of Louise Gluck in *Wild Iris*, but more than that, I think of Rilke again. When he was secretary to Rodin, the sculptor sent this inwardly obsessed poet to the Paris zoo, to force himself to look out.

With a new MS, diagnosis, Gill took on this manuscript and set the goal of completing it within a calendar year. She had the good instinct or impulse to frame her work in the healing plants, a life-affirming and outward-calling project. She succeeded within that time frame, yet the poems seem well-seasoned and crafted.

If there were a country called Diagnosis, she is the Poet Laureate, a job she'd never want, but an occasion she rises to with dignity, wild talent, and humor.

The medicinal herbs serve as metaphor, persona, anchor, or companion.
Not one poem is predictable. I'd suggest, as the poet did to me, that you
read the poems without the notes first, straight through. *Mortar & Pestle*
isn't only about illness. It's harsh, honest life itself and these poems are the
good medicine:

> "I forage for opportunities
>
> to practice the alchemy that transforms
> desperation into brightness"
>   —Cnicus benedictus | **Blessed Thistle**
>
> "What's protected is ardor"
>   —Crataegus oxyacantha | **Hawthorn**
>
> "Now when the sun sets
> my pupils flower
> and I can see
> less of this body
> and more of the world.
> Aha."
>   —Datura stramonium | **Jimsonweed**

I dare you to sit down and give yourself to this book. It comes with a
meditative and spiritual imperative. Reading Lisa Gill connected me to
the day, my own body, and to the natural world. I felt the lines of the
poems as the lines of a drawing in a field guide or herbal. There are jokes
and word play tuned to the frequency of each plant, insider asides, mottos,
and mantras. I found myself turning the pages as the poems escalated
and strengthened, wondering where's she was going next and willing to
follow:

> " All is plush and passing."
>   —**The Complaint**
>
> " We have the ability to *altar* each other."
>   —Piper Methysticium | **Kava**
>
>
> " A mortar and pestle with lips."
>   —Piper Methysticum | **Kava**

Indeed it is the language and energy of the ecstatics, rubbed across feminism, all the more remarkable when you consider the physical circumstances of the writing. Neruda and Mirabai run off together. Anne Sexton meets the Buddha on the road. Emily D. steps out with Dylan Thomas. These poems crush and macerate the best of the inner against the best of outer. Lisa Gill has paid her dues, done the work, and we get to harvest "Fifty-Two Consolations" of healing herbs in *Mortar & Pestle*. I hope and pray she is read by many, especially those who can use a dose of life force.

Joan Logghe

Joan Logghe is the author of *Rice* (Tres Chicas), *Twenty Years in Bed with the Same Man* (La Alameda), *Blessed Resistance* (Mariposa), *Sofia* (La Alameda), *What Makes a Woman Beautiful* (Pennywhistle), and the anthologies *Catch Our Breath: Writing from the Heart of AIDS* (Mariposa) and *Another Desert: Jewish Poetry of New Mexico* (Sherman Asher), edited with Miriam Sagan; she is the recipient of a National Endowment for the Arts in Poetry and the Barbara Deming Memorial Money for Women grant; she lives in La Puebla, New Mexico.

Bloodroot | Potentilla tormentilla

What's yellow flowered rises from a root so red, so tapered and sap flowing, picture a finger bent under a blade and expect to see some blood. Here is agony and the elixir, desire with its queasy stomach, the tongue pressing a sore tooth, even the upstairs rectory where fear and longing tremble.

This is the dirt: you want to see blood, at least a little bit, because who doesn't pray for the opportunity to get under the skin of something? We all hunger to scratch the surface, dig down, uproot a little flesh, take hold with five fingers and maybe concoct panacea, glimpse God, or simply maintain control of every mortar and pestle in the vicinity so we'll know when and why rhizomes are bruised.

And if blood spills secrets from political tyrannies into economic back alleys, or if an accidental encounter with a sharp object or some average prick causes us to stumble upon some re-tellable scarlet anecdote, we should remember that the double helix is a ladder descending into primordial sludge.

Here between earth and heaven, mineshaft and the great hole in the ozone, we dabble in the art of becoming vulnerable before becoming dead.

Even one solitary bead of blood can take root in the imagination because so long as enough blood flows, the human mind can't be corralled like some ewe or a plucked daisy in a dry pasture. Thoughts creep into woods where any curve can signify the tip of a pinky or underside of a woman's breast.

Moreover, a bead's not all over some heath, rather suspended in time and space, fragile, poised as if to defy the laws of gravity, so one drop illuminates our desire to make the amorphous tangible and to make the tangible into a tincture that will never putrefy.

If a single bead was once upon a time sweet, self-contained, innocent, now we can't root out the daily deluge of spatters, smears, splats, spurt-n-gush.

We must contend with both the force of what's been dammed up and our memory of what happens to any drip after the inevitable encounter with a glass slide, syringe, or cutting board.

(Four bright petals make a Maltese cross if you shoulder the prospect of wilting.)

There's always surface tension. Sometimes it gives us a fat lip; sometimes we get one to press our mouths to. Water rises above the edge of a full cup in an arc bordering on ecstatic spill.

If one person's wound is another's breakthrough, we all choose what to cherish, what to blot.

The Complaint

With a body tethered to gravity
with a body tethered to time
a body tethered
and a mind
strapped into form by flesh,
                              flail.

                              Or, extol
the virtues of vulnerability.

Here is the daily argh
the flat gasp
the hacking cough
the charlie horse
the spit
and the star-shaped stones.

Here is the hemorrhage
the mucus
the split lip
the black eye
the gout.

Here is the biological clock

that pressures us to do anything
or at least reproduce a good time.

This is the fever dream
the interruption
the unscheduled
the loss of control.

This is the kick
—minimal transcendence—
the quick and undulating instinct
of the cell of the organism
to preserve by whatever means possible
the body.

This is a riddle on a skeleton.
Existential popsicle.
Lollygag.

I begin my days slowly
as if to cull any last knowledge from sleep

as if there's time enough to wake up
later

as if I could ever wake up completely
and solve something:

      the latest dilemma,
      the nearest quandary,
      the fervent hope.

I would like to understand.

If not understand, then accept
(or at least not resent)
this fleshy apparition that constitutes
one lifetime.

Living grit and impossibilities.
Emotional nuance.

I think neuropeptides.
I think a sunset, a garden, a house fire.
I think popping a pill will help.
I think the pins and needles stuck in my left foot
are a distraction from some true course, some calling,
some less physically dictated life I was supposed to lead.

I think I'm wrong.
I think I ought to know better.
I think a flawed body is a good idea.
     A keystone.
     The arch of my foot.
     The apple in my mouth.
The nuisance that'll school me proper.

But the brain in the skull still wants
to fix it
to make it better
to make afflictions go away.

Oh for the assuage, the balm, the placate.

Here is my hindrance, my hunger, my vestigial hope.

     I imagine solace curled up fetal
     somewhere within my grasp
     if I'm willing to reach out.

Beyond the confines of this thing
I pass through time and space in,
the world is plush.

Rephrase: this thing I pass through
is part of a plush world.

Rephrase: all is plush and passing.

Right here, chollas and prickly pear,
four o'clocks and pepperweed,
a hatchet and bacteria.

See how the moon has risen
before the sun could set and
obscure the blue grama?

Arc over arc.

Bounty:
          Organs.
          Arms and legs.
          Fingers and opposable thumbs.
I pick up the concept of symmetry
and toy with loss and recovery
joy and despair
the mind and the body
the body and the world.

Duality rages on
but at least I'm conflicted
hold the knife in one hand
the poultice in the other.
One body.

Mirror mirror.

My mouth looks like a maw.
It is. A toothed thing always
tonguing words or eating.
Always hunger.
And the appetites.

Kiss me.

Press your body on my body
and we will be the picture
of imperfections.

I can forget how often
I can forget myself
when it's late at night
and I'm still confronting
the way I used to take
my body for granted.

Bicycle rides and insomnia.

Vehicle for whatever
disease began to develop
years before the diagnosis.

And now fear.
And now fret.

I didn't want a nagging body.

Welcome to the bowels of desire
where everything begins with
what you don't want and ends
with an awareness of what you wasted.

God help me cut the clamor.
Or love the dissonance.

Realize: The mind is worse off than the body.

We can live with boils and ulcers and arthritis.
We can live with hep C and cancers and multiple sclerosis.
We can live with just about anything up until we don't—
because we have to.

But the mind is still wrapped up
in some utopian myth high in the branches
of the brain and cries out
                        and cries out
                                and cries out
longing for some laying hands conversion
that would exchange hypodermic needles
for any semblance of plain faith.

This is the squawking to attend to.

So give me any materia medica
and I will concoct something
before the knockdown.

If I can't count on having the right afflictions,
the soothe-able ones,
the there-there,
quick fix
pep-talkables
I can count on those arcs as universal forms
that I can hold to different light.
This pits resonance against alienation
and I'm out
in the next available reverie
watching a mother's hand stroking a grown child's hair.

And then I'm out on the mesa
cursing a central nervous system that requires solace.

Revere anger.
Because it is not a lesion.
Because it is a tool.

I could carve canyons this way
and you bet waters would rage also.
White caps.

Gray hairs.
There are so many things I'm not afraid of.

Inside the claustrophobia of the sickbed brews
a curiosity that eventually won't be contained.

(Recovery helps.) But here is courage.

The search.
The futile quest.
The battle the mind fights.

Call it "coming to terms."
Everything gets labeled.
      Endocrine,
      Vascular,
      Gastrointestinal,
      Autonomic
      Coffee pot,
      Dog,
      Family photo.

When you get the first inkling of genetic order
and inherit the tendency to blame
the (non)sense phase begins.

Every which why.

God
bad luck
the latitude
the glass of milk
the early trauma
or the recent trauma
lentils or wheat or corn
ingratitude or repression
spent weapons in the forest
asbestos in the old school building
that drop of mercury held in the palm
the old swimming hole the wrong place
the wrong time the wrong predisposition
toothpaste or karma or not abiding the food
pyramid clothing line marketing schemes turn

back to the real dirt
the better skinny
and say: what now?

It's dawn already and I haven't slept. What now?
1000 suns brighten through gaps in juniper twigs.
I am enlightened. Or my window is.

I am slightly delirious.

Any body has limits that can be bypassed.
The edge is so enticing.
I get stabbed touching the purple thistle
missing a whole night's sleep.
Another appointment.

Where is my common sense?
Gone like an appendix?
Or wisdom teeth?
Or maybe gone to seed.

The remedy might be something simple.
The remedy might be a right thought.
A grain of rice as opposed to a pebble.

Perhaps I can catch it or glean it
from some old text by Pliny or Dioscorides
under an entry headed What Will Fix You Up.

As if health were just another fling.
A blind romance.
A date.

Once I didn't think of myself as a riddle
with a mouth and an anus.
Once I didn't think in terms of parts
or their utility.
I didn't think.
I didn't have to.

Yet I don't want to go back
to the blissful stupor
recline in the armchair
as if there were no as ifs.

So set my feet on the earth
and my body about its business
thump and gurgle

inhale
exhale
blink

Everything is gone.

This is how it works.

Golden

1	wondering
1	if
2	the number
3	of current lesions
5	in my brain is more
8	random than petal structure or if small deaths
13	on my MRI also correlate to the Fibonacci sequence or a black-eyed Susan

1	calla
1	lily
2	or euphorbia
3	I bypassed trillium
5	wanted to stop with columbine
8	but visible even on my first brain scan
13	delphinium and larkspur as if what's freshly gathered is this tendency to accumulate
21	so for every aster I will watch the progression of this disease as if the pattern were beholden to natural order

1	pineapple
1	pinecone
2	cactus spines
3	poplar wisdom enough
5	to fill the shell of every
8	Archimedes spiral into despair with transformation and growth
13	only the naturalist observation of each stage will illuminate how we are intertwined
21	with other lives where there is exponential potential to rotate one's ordinary thinking a few degrees clockwise to counter the illusion
34	of isolation by letting our apathy decay and make fodder for real curiosity until one day or another MRI scan the ratio of life being lived versus life spent contemplating death will be golden

Fifty-Two Consolations

Achillea millefolium | **Yarrow**

I'm looking for my great weakness.
I see a thousand things.

I suspect my entire body
is composed of Achilles' heels.

Like a Warhol. Picture cells
replicating the same-strained DNA.

A thousand things go wrong.
And yet this is nothing.

A plant can make me sweat
or break a fever.

I am perfectly vulnerable
as if dipped in the Rio Grande.

I suspect my body is composed
of everything discernible

and undiscernible.
I overlook a thousand things.

The contractions have started.
I can't, I won't, I didn't notice.

I'm birthing regret.
Don't staunch this.

Agave parryi | **Century Plant**

I walk in the desert
and find the hours succulent
fat with minutes.

Close to the ground
leaves hold water tight.
I drink up the propitiousness.

This is what intoxicates me:
time
before disease blossoms.

I've got decades
a century or another month
until some garish flare.

String the hammock
so I can unhurry the afternoon.
I'm in no rush to the spectacular.

Flowering can be fatal.
An end. I want to enjoy
the means.

Aloe barbadensis | **Aloe**

From drought I have learned
to wrap my body
in the written record of water.
Papyrus monsoons
whet the blade of the knife
that will split
the fat leaf of the sky lengthwise.

How lovely the scorched and scalded.
How lovely the bemoaning.
How lovely.

Like this desert.
Like dirt downtrodden by cattle.
Like the resurrection of resilience.

Survival is nothing glamorous,
Cleopatraed.
It's spiked as my determination
to wait out
every dry spell with a vengeance,
the sun burning
clean the blade readied in my hand.

Amaranthus hypochondriacus | **Love-Lies-Bleeding**

(Honesty is all that's unwithering.)

So I asked if I had to get pregnant
to get your attention back.

Flat out.
Hysterical.
Hypothetical. You
                said no.

So here love lies bleeding.
The way I want to be in your bed.

Angelica archangelica | **Angelica**

I need to press my body into soil
beside running water or invoke someone.

The monsoons have drawn back
into the heavens, so help me, Michael.

The land around my house is dry
and I am tired

of spending my days alone
building blood and thinking.

Is this the great battle?
A quiet woman hounded by her head?

Today if I go outside I could stumble
upon the bodies of Moses and Eve.

Commandments and temptation
are the same thing: foliage.

I'm confounded.
Show me where to dig.

Arnica montana | **Arnica**

Send a telegram:
      Goethe drank tea.

This matters as much as anything.
Gossip as vasodilator.

      We share with other humans
      the desire to soothe what ails.

Tonight this matters because my heart
aches in a way leopard's bane can't help.

The last thing I want to hear about is spots
when my MRI is plagued with them.

So tell me Goethe drank tea.
I can sit down with this knowledge

and pretend empathy
or at least grasp the yellow slab of fear

and give it hope's tsk tsk
the regular reprimand of resignation

to flesh.

Artemesia frigida | **Wormwood**

Today's bitterness was lost
on the mountain.

           Or found
in another silver-haired form.

So I became an old woman
when I got sick a year ago.

The mountain doesn't care
if I'm despondent.

Or delusional—
years didn't pass.

It's just midsummer again,
anniversary of my thwarted.

A season's growth can foil
any pouting.

I've been hanging my head
day after day.

The picture of grief
           or any picture

of inclined blossoms.
Earth could be my rapture,

the old woman new growth
sprung up

to acknowledge loss
and what's impending

eventually. I'll get older
than the illusion I can't expel.

Betula alba | **White Birch**

Let the strip of white bark be
a tactile void,
a place for today's inexpressibles.

I feel lost
and content not to know the way
back.

The hard stones I dropped down
to mark the trail dissolved
under the weight of falling leaves.

My awareness
of everything left behind each choice
pacifies something.

As if sacrifices mean nothing
is wasted.

What's right and what's wrong
become irrelevant.

There is only the next open space
and the occasional opportunity
to pause.

Calendula officinalis | **Marigold**

Here's a bright spot.
A wound packed with blossoms.
Healing requires pluck.

After any conflict
flowers get drafted from the earth
                antithesis of uniforms

                beatitudes of color.
Cultivate consolation year round because,
face the sun,

things fester.
My lover brought me marigolds
                after our last scrape.

                I'd been slighted
and was stewing a meager pot of broth
on the kitchen stove.

When he came in
his hands full of flowers I knew
                we'd adorn each other.

                And the soup.
Even the virgin in the upturned tub
got a garland.

Something was righted.
Assuage is not a romantic word
                but *calendula* is

                a balm of sorts.
A wound packed with blossoms
beats a wound.

Calluna vulgaris | **Heather**

You have a shovel,
I have a knife,
it's time we lie
on a mattress made
from a hillside
and listen for music
from underground.
Your subconscious
never lacks for
an instrument while
mine is rife with
heaths and moors.
So honey, dig up
your pan pipes and
I will lie down on
memory. Together
let's play shanties,
even dirges. Late
summer nights
macerating flowers
for absolution,
we'll sleep in tune
with everything
burgeoning.
In the morn,
ruddy-faced
and rising,
we can kiss
the hours
we love
adieu.

Capsicum annum | **Cayenne**

Let's not have another
humdrum supper.

Domesticity doesn't suit
my taste.

A staid version of coupling
sticks in my head.

Meat and potatoes
from childhood.

I can't escape my revulsion
against that marriage.

Even the routines
were taken for granted.

Prove to me
we're not becoming that

or some other disparagement
of imagination.

Blacken your body and
make my capillaries dilate

until heat moves me
moves my fear

right out of the cells
that imprison memory.

Today I could destroy
everything

resembling a house or a table.
Tell me why not.

Centella asiatica | **Gotu Kola**

This is what I like to do:
clutch the edges of schism and pull.

Apart is alluring.

If I have a propensity to leper myself,
it's selfish. The satisfaction of the pariah
is manifold.

>   Indignation
>   followed by
>   unharangued.

>   Think *untouchable*
versus *untouched*.

Both hurt.
One can be accepted with some finality.
As if the work is done.

But nothing's over.

I pack the schism with fan-shaped leaves
and attempt to cross.

Cnicus benedictus | **Blessed Thistle**

Blessed are the unknown trajectories.

Charlemagne shot an arrow into the sky.
I watched meteors.

He aimed for nothing or some cloud
and let sharp find sharp.

I looked without looking
and found light everywhere peripheral.

If thistles banished the plague
what Charlemagne plundered was faith.

The stars of fate are not constellations
we know.

The legend began with a dream
of relinquishing control

and being receptive to the unintentional.
I forage for opportunities

to practice the alchemy that transforms
desperation into brightness.

Crataegus oxyacantha | **Hawthorn**

Here the heart is an old world garden,
four plots separated by hedges.

Cloister, cavern, cistern, well.

The only arrhythmia is a girl skipping
in the right atrium.

Anteroom, arbor, tree fort, loo.

Blood rushes to her cheeks,
bright as berries.

Barbershop, pantry, under the bed.

No matter life is prickly,
She cultivates an affinity for thorns.

Ward off, ward off, beat it, go.

And prunes the space between thorns,
the chance openings.

Oh, come here, I'd like to, yes.

What's protected is ardor,
the heart with its various pleasures.

Cloister, cavern, cistern, well.

Datura stramonium | **Jimsonweed**

When I lost my equilibrium
I found the ground
and what grows there.

A trumpet of guffaws.

As if I'd misplaced
my attention. Simple error.
Egregious.

I broke a sweat
grappling with gravity
with God.

Initiated into overblown
blossoms and seeds
of anything

my body became
a distant horizon
I reached weeks later.

Now when the sun sets
my pupils flower
and I can see

less of this body
and more of the world.
Aha.

Echinacea angustifolia | **Echinacea**

The hedgehog in me has curled up.
Again.

The fact of spines leaves me crestfallen
                as petals on a coneflower.

I don't want to guard against you.
I don't want to get burned.

Inadvertents accumulated chaffing my skin.
The thick and the thin is hurt.

Instinct kicked in
and erected a buffer. Between you and me,
                      already
protected space is narrow as a quandary.

I don't want to guard against you.
I want to take the live coal into my mouth
                   and smolder.
                   Safely.
                   Vulnerable
has become so vulnerable.
Again.

          For a while,
     leave me
             rounded
        unto myself.

Time erodes everything,
                 even defenses,
         especially defenses.

Fallugia paradoxa | **Apache Plume**

Today I don't regret
binding myself to the soil.

I found my deliverance
in the piñon juniper belt.

Plumes.

Ordinary life feathering
into the mythic.

A shrub up against
the erosion of my confidence.

Lately I've made decisions
standing on the edge of an arroyo.

Flash of insight,
flood of emotion.

I can still get carried away
by the idea of loss

instead of what's found.
So I walk the irrevocable path

tremulous and recently
bruised

hoping to find any sign
that acceptance is not misplaced.

Filipendula ulmaria | **Meadowsweet**

After the rainstorm
I went out
late last night
to watch the clouds
recede.

This is respite.

Stars multiplying
and the sky
regaining
depth.

Now
the earth is wet
and wildspringing.

My perspective
also.

As if I didn't have to
worry.

Or believe in disease.

As if I was obligated
to daydream.

Relief
seems so simple.

Some meadow
and the passage
of clouds,
the chance
to stretch
out.

Ginkgo biloba | **Ginkgo**

Climb this tree.

Leaves will beat against your brow
and clouds overhead
will mushroom.

Fret.

Many people fail to remember
many things. Whole cities
have been wiped out.

Let grief rise. High
in the branches of any gingko
you will find the epicenter of sadness.

Cherish this grief
as you would cherish a silver apricot.

Or, pick one leaf
and press it against your forehead.
Find solace.

Rift is not the whole story.
The old impressions of division
will fade.

A finger
can trace the larger union
between self and other.

Fan this knowledge.

Picture a grandfather walking
with his grandson.

Picture a lover stroking
a woman's hair.

Picture yourself
with a leaf stuck to your forehead.

Laugh.

Clamber down and kneel.
This is a temple.
Pray or begin digging.

Let the dirt cloister your hands.

You'll find fossils
from the Cretaceous Era, roots
going back centuries.

Time gets under your nails.

The earth is fecund, ripe
with life and death,
more recent litter.

Yesterday is there,
as is tomorrow, curled up
like a crustacean.

Everyone deserves this
tactile familiarity.
Cup the earth.

Hold what you can.

Glycyrrhiza glabra | **Licorice**

Four years I have been spurned by solace.
I turn and turn in my bed.

Grief masks my perennial companion
yet my thoughts are stalked by purple blossoms

and pairs of oval leaves.
This is longing. Every day I bury another desire

deep in the dirt around licorice roots
and ask Osiris to open Tutankhamun's tomb

for the harvest in autumn. Bring on the plow.
I have an affinity for sweet wood.

Even a carved ibex
will want to clamber mountains. Eventually

everything unrequited is simply unrequited.
Yearning sticks in my throat.

Closed lips, open wounds.
Bring me my tobacco.

Or lay me down in the bushes
and arrange fifty sugar cubes on my belly.

Let something besides my body shrivel
and provide succor.

Grindelia aphanactis | **Gumweed**

Today sprang onto the calendar
like a gumplant on the roadside.

Unremarkable.

Sixteen hours with nothing
but the smallest snatch of color.

I put the whole pronged cup
of sentiment in my mouth anyway.

                  So all day
I've been chewing on the idea
of relative brightness.

The sun versus the color yellow.
Cultivated or wild.

Weed shouldn't be
              a four letter word.

I catch judgment
in some people's inflection.

It makes me want to hack up
my own derision and let fly
              a loogey
on the old hierarchies that make
one day worth more than another.

Sometimes I just want to love
              the common
the ordinary promiscuity of hours
and whatever can catch my attention.

Gutierrezia sarothrae | **Snakeweed**

I walk among
rounds of yellow that
cows won't graze.

What thrives
in disturbed places
is resistance—

bright light
of protest and
non-cooperation.

This is the snakebite
that will transform
the culture

or at least survive
and gradually
get stronger.

I amass confidence
in my legs
and quiet in my heart—

against odds,
alongside,
with.

Hamamelis virginiana | **Witch Hazel**

Here's a switch.

I've always had the ability to berate
my bare back or make a broom to ride
my faults into a corner of my skull

but now I put both hands
on a forked branch
and dowse.

The tug of imagination is subtle.

In the sun yellow petals spider about
while fruit ejects seeds with a snap.
Nothing about snapping is subtle.

An auditory eclipse.
Ten yards later you get the dirt
on impact.

Impulse is distilled.

Welts rise up
and receptivity sinks in.
This is a crooked reverie

where I search for relief
from one inflammation
and cultivate another.

Hydrastis canadensis | **Goldenseal**

Here is the wax seal closing
the envelope on yesterday.

The puckered scar reveals
enough.

I don't need to hear about
every microbe and parasite
that thrived on your body.

I don't want to.

I place a single inedible berry
in each ear canal.

Give me the myth of a present
clean-severed from the past.

Or supply me with hope
that demands on your mind
won't always stem from old roots.

God,
you could say this to me too.

You should.

In the interest of fair trade,
I'll take the berries out of my ears
and listen.

Maybe I'll even bury my head
on your chest and catch sound
of your current heartbeat.

This pact's golden.

Hypericum perforatum | **St. John's Wort**

Sometimes the aerial parts are useful.

I place John the Baptist's severed head
in a sachet under my pillow at night
so my dreams spread like goatweed.

Picture crusades of yellow flowers.

If I pluck the petals and press them
between my fingers, I draw blood.
Soft imprint of red iconography.

This is a reversal of fortune.

Lately heads are rolling all over
the internet. People are shocked but
death's always personal, named.

John isn't alone on June 24th.

We build freeways wide as gashes
and then fill them with trucks, duck
responsibility for consumerism.

Warrior's wounds grow on roadsides.

The harvest brings in bales of grief,
stacks them on the bureau. Oh criminy.
Apathy's the demon to chase out.

Try to keep your head, your humanity.

This bouquet's a bundle of sunlight
so bright welts will rise up on your skin—
the pain of the world in relief. Feel it.

Juniperus monosperma | **One-Seed Juniper**

If it weren't for junipers, the land
around my house would blow away.

Funny thought.
I don't want to live alone anymore.

Here is how the scales don't tip
too far.

Short trees, long shadows.

Coyotes have somewhere to hide
and cows go around.

How to accommodate predators
and the usual decimation.

I balance a berry on a fingertip.
Mash was the first impulse

but precarious invites communion
or at least curiosity.

So I attempt the awkward.
When the berry drops, I watch it

fall.
Then pick it back up.

Lavandula officinalis | **Lavender**

Tonight sweeten the passage of grief.

I held my cat all day.

If every loss could be so merciful
and close,

>   a hand stroking the belly
>   as the needle approaches
>   feeling the final heart spike.

Picture the moment you close the pages
of some book around a blossom,
memory pressing everything.

I am saddened past weeping

or I am past weeping
into the next throes

where I contemplate every old parting
that was ever arranged by death

>   and strew flowers
>   and strew flowers
>   and strew flowers.

Lobelia inflata | **Lobelia**

Every time my vision snags
on a panicle of reds, I gasp.

For that breathless instant
the oldest tether is broken.

My mind is wrenched free
from time and the too-steady

rhythm of inhalations and
exhalations. Breathing clods

along most days like a work-
horse. I could get bored

or ungrateful if it weren't for
the gaps. One day I'll be

a different kind of breathless.
Ask the dead if I'm morbid

or simply practical when
I don't purge mortality

from my awareness of what
pleasure means to my body.

Marrubium vulgare | **Horehound**

I walked the bitter roadside
refusing to pass over
what runoff nourished.

The environment around
the fast-driven cut deserves
to be seen

as the picture of thriving
despite and today this
is my intent

to maintain a quiet resilience
against the hacking progress
of the body's dismantling

as if simply creating
another ecosystem
where despair comes down

like rain redirected
into unexpected channels
of exuberance.

Matricaria recutita | **Chamomile**

Some plants thrive even when walked on.

Resilience can seem so dowdy,
so hard pressed,
so forgiving.

It's not like I want to accept every slight
or boot on my skull.
I'm stubborn.

Look at my brow.
Still knit.
You should be able to read between the lines.

When did I learn to resist recovery?
In the womb?
After eating an apple?

Tonight give me a tablespoon of temperate
and teach me
that healing is not succumbing.

I can swallow it—
a rotten day with terminal flowers
anyhow.

Look at my brow.
I am unknitting a sad myth.
Pride.

There are better things to consecrate:
modest resurrections
and different kinds of uprisings.

Tomorrow I may try plain speech.

Medicago sativa | **Alfalfa**

Comely field,
you are my green convalescence.

Thigh high in buffalo grass,
I bound.

I eat up
this vision of the open sky

and what's sprung up beneath
my feet.

Purple blossoms
with long histories of delight

and deer.
You have tapped into the wealth

of my wonder.
Small days ending with long walks.

Melissa officinalis | **Lemon Balm**

The rain stopped
but water keeps coming
from miles back on the mountain.

Silver threads.

I want to stitch
the cracked clouds back together
and let it pour some more.

Already I can't see you so why not
let the world flood and the land run off
between my fingers.

The monsoons speak to me.

I am flowing back into myself, I am
moving boulders and washing out roads.

The distance from here to anywhere
expands exponentially.

Whether this is solace or grief, I don't know
except I am inconsolable.

In the morning bring me balm.
Or, if you still can't reach me,
send out a solitary honey bee.

When it nuzzles the sprig of small
white blossoms in my hand, perhaps
I'll believe in something again.

Mentha piperita | **Peppermint**

I've been letting the wrong things go
to my head.

        Thoughts like dog bites
and wasp stings. Or turds I can't identify
as those of a mouse my cat caught.

My body's become inhospitable.
To me.

      My head aches and the past
      is a rotten analgesic. Okay
      it's only been two days since
      I drank juleps on the porch

            but I need to belch.
            A cosmic dispelling
            of every sad myth or
            cup of coffee I cling to.

I'm being candid.
Dish.

        The air needs to be cleared.
Somehow, I got to warm up to myself.

Oenothera biennis | **Evening Primrose**

When I was sliced in half by a mirror
and my body turned against my body,
you were my sun drop.

How could I say stay?

Four breasts and two heads. Disease
slated every night for another bruise
to my nerves and ego. I thought you'd

                let go.

The light faded to four yellow petals.
One embrace armed me with evening
instead of nightfall.

Diagnosis shrank to a sprig.

                You stayed
and we curled up on sandy soil. Dunes
riddled with wind and disbelief.

Now in our second year, I can see
the seed you've held between your lips.

And I can accept a sliver of the moon
at sunrise.

Birds call.
I promise, birds call.

Passiflora incarnata | **Passionflower**

There was nothing maypop
about our last supper.

The fruit on the table suffered
the consequences of lips—
appetites and harsh words.

We died back to the ground.
Then got into bed to weep.

Moonlight through curtains
illuminated something dormant
in our bereft. Worry lifted.

You spread flesh-colored petals
all around my body.

We touched gentle and adamant
as tendrils of a vine, pulling
ourselves towards each other.

Love is long-clambering.
Hardship part of the trellis.

Every day we suffer
the wonder of lips—
kiss and consequence.

Piper methysticum | **Kava**

I have taken anxiety into my mouth
and chewed it.
A mortar and pestle with lips.
I speak bowls.
Transformation can be cultivated
this simply.
A bare-breasted woman spitting.

Most of the time I wear sackcloth.
Or used to.
Tension mounted our conversations.
A cold infusion.
We'd fallen prey to the ballistics
of outside squabbles.
The sheer hackery of modern life.

There's mourning and there's refuge.
We forget.
Indulgence is as simple as an embrace.
Together
even our muscles lounge like cats
after a kill.
We have the ability to *altar* each other.

Rhamnus purshianus | **Cascara Sagrada**

Let pass the oldest grievance.
Let pass the recent slight.
Let go the shame and the morass

So I have had tantrums.
So I have lost arguments.
So I have turned red-faced and stuttering.

So there is a septic tank in my back yard.

When I feel stuck
I sit by the leach field.

It's plush there.

Peristalsis is not so easy for the mind
as the body but I encourage the habit.

Clutch and release.
Recall and forget.
Thank the bacteria.

Even breaking down vanity
purges something.

There is so much crap
on the way to the smallest catharsis.

If we are lucky,
there is one hour in each day
when we are temporarily emptied
and open
to the next possibility.

Ruta graveolens | **Rue**

I want to cleanse myself of misconceptions.
Fertile mind,
incubus.

Grief has had its way with me.

I rue the day spent sleeping,
then rue my waking hours.

Yesterday there were sad birds
on both sides of my bedroom window.
One in my hand, one waiting
perched on the evergreen.

I set free
the desire for happiness.

Expectation is the insemination of regret.
I can't have this.

Scutellaria lateriflora | **Skullcap**

From the side of the stem
where blossoms aren't,
a snarl.

Low-throttled, guttural—
                    and opportunistic.

My voice escaped the pen
where I'd quarantined it.

Now every breath's gouged
by teeth.

I curse
the indiscriminate riverbank.

Gray matter waters the worst
thoughts, sets fear prowling.

My amygdalae glow.
Two eyes I can't stare down.

Three years ago I wrestled
seeds into the stubborn soil:
                    hoodwort,
                    madcap,
                    mental hospital.

Now at least
I can reap perspective.

On the side of the stem
where the snarl isn't,
blossoms.

Silybum marianum | **Milk Thistle**

White veins on green leaves.
          As if the Virgin Mary
accidentally gave suck to a thistle.

Prickly,
the idea that spilled breast milk
from the mother of the Son of God
might nourish us
            this way.

Pliny said,
it's not worth the effort to boil.

We're lazy.
And we make mistakes.
Share needles or become a nurse
        and get stuck.

Even a tattoo
can leave us contemplating God
and the viral load.

Talk about bile.
Between poverty and helplessness,
     faith gets jaundiced.

Once we thought we'd live forever,
life a perpetual red blossom.

Now we look for solace but pick
an amanita mushroom
            or a bottle.
Things go to seed.

Here is asylum.
          As if the Virgin Mary
accidentally gave suck to a thistle.

Symphytum officinale | **Comfrey**

The word *marriage*
makes me want to boil
a pot of water with ass ear.

Any two pieces of flesh
can be glued together.

Sticky hodgepodge.

I worry even though
we came together
like a clean break.

No ceremony.

We just set our bones
on the same bed.

Now we've grown together.

Already I feel an itch
under the hardening cast.

I'm ready to crack
routine in half and see
what we've become.

Tanacetum parthenium | **Feverfew**

I caught myself on the way to a migraine.

I saw the linoleum floor coming
and thought twice:

> Retching is too lonely.
> Retching is too lonely.

This is ridiculous.

Yesterday I knocked on my dog's head
and he barked. My own skull is hammered
like that.

I am the bane,
the plague, the scourge.

I pulled all the petals off the flowers
before I started asking any questions.

Love me? Love me null.

I have the luck of the self-flagellating.
Bald bouquet in my hand and whether
in my head.

Reel.

The sky pitches.
I steady myself on fallen petals.

Today I don't feel like retching.

Taraxacum officinale | **Dandelion**

When trepidation goes to seed
even the wind wishes me well,

dispersing the once bright knots
of fear with breath.

How common the exhalation.
How exultant.

To release the turbid
and propagate simple hope.

Today I want for nothing
because I want again everything.

Ordinary longing,
my appetite has returned

with a roar and a prayer.
Pat a big cat

or a priest's shorn head.
I am playing children's games,

the serious work of distraction,
the work of wishing well.

Thelesperma filifolium | **Cota**

Yesterday my end
of the conversation
was threadbare.
What could I say?
It's monsoon season—
fluidity is reserved
for the desert
and the rising toads.
Even when waters
flood new channels
across the valley,
there is no excess.
Evaporation is fast.
The desert is always
tightlipped here,
withholding color
from the first glance
as if sparse is
a second language
we have to learn
not to be confounded.
So last night I sat
quiet but you stayed
bright as any tightly
bound bundle of tiny
yellow blossoms.
Finally I couldn't
help but pull a
blue-green string
from the hem of
my jeans shorts
and tie a slipknot
around your fingers.

Ulmus fulva | **Slippery Elm**

Everything slips through my fingers.
Whole trees

succumb to disease
and are removed from the pharmacopoeia.

Some days helplessness is a companion
instead of an adversary.

I simply watch
all these passages towards death thinking

perhaps we are made to be confounded.
I can't even hold

all the minutes
in a single daydream of health or longevity

so why not throw my arms up and welcome
the next blight

as a chance
to practice the unclutching of everything.

Urtica dioica | **Stinging Nettle**

Our days are deeply serrate
cut to the quick and the dowdy.

I'd pull a knife and slice off
everything extraneous except
these are ordinary fetters.

We are unfree and will be.

So this requires a different
intervention, counter-intuitive.

Sometimes one irritation
can be soothed by another.

Today I was placated by hail.
A deafening racket. Listening
was the only endeavor possible.

I felt hammered into peace.

The sting of acceptance
was brief so tomorrow I may
beat my body with nettles.

In the face of so many prickly
contenders for attention,
I should pick some for myself.

Vaccinium myrtillus | **Bilberry**

If you pick whortleberries in the dark
you might pluck out the eyes from ghosts.

World War II wasn't long ago.

A few aggrieved dead
must still haunt jam-eaters.

Lick your fingers.

Night bombing raids were
as good as
the afternoon tea with scones–

provided,
pilots skipped marmalade and loaded up
with jelly.

Microcirculation makes for
macrophantasmagoria.

On huckleberry,
they became the *Flying Retinas*.
Bombs away.

It's clear
sight and the application of sight
are two different things.

Possibly shades of gray were always
striking
but war ripens medicine for the reaper.

Here is the blue-black fruit.

Valeriana officinalis | **Valerian**

Phu, something stinks.
Scratch the surface and
my cat would roll here.

The party line is quell:
all-heal.
Don't show coffins
or photographs of dead.

Be happy. War happens
in other countries and
you don't wake up
in the night whimpering
to an air raid siren.
Rest well.

This is America.
Restless legs can be
soldiered off or couched
in front of the latest
pied piper to garner
an umbrella of ratings.

Even the shellshocked
and the menstrual
get calmed by copycat
pharmaceuticals.
Purr.

Dig a bit.
Expose the musk.
Say, Phu.

Verbascum thapsus | **Mullein**

My lack of faith is a spire,
a towering biennial.

Mockingbirds flock to me.

Last year I thought
the rosette was nothing
but a rosette—basal leaves.

Everything was foreshortened
and stalled in dirt.

Moribund fate.

So I pulled the wool over
every season.

I thought I'd winter the worst
by readying the wick for the pyre.

Now everything's up in the air.

Or at least there's a spire
where there was nothing
but a rosette.

How many times must I forget
about change?

Mockingbirds flock to me.

Vitex agnus-castus | **Chaste Tree**

I'm on my own,
an unbidden novitiate into a long night
without you.

Absence is a rudimentary cloister.

Without monks or nuns
to make frustration look beatified,
I'm at a loss
to understand this doctrine.

> Separation
> as opposed to estrangement.

As if I've forgotten how to be alone
unexpectedly
though I kept this vigil for years

and we keep separate houses
with schedules like anaphrodisiacs.

Tonight there is no consolation
only endurance of a few chaste hours
and the memory of lips parting.

> Separation
> as opposed to estrangement.

Yucca glauca | **Yucca**

I don't always like going out.
My roots are part animal.
Like parts of animals
easily displaced by coyotes.

From the dirt
to the sky on the high mesa
is a journey of some violence.

An upending
by hoof or snout or shovel.

It makes me froth.

I don't want to be unearthed
completely.

Staying grounded is crux.
Existence in the desert
can be fragile.

The elements are ravaging.
I can handle the arduous
and still find a way to bloom
if left to myself.

Zingiber officinale | **Ginger**

I come to you from dirt in the Garden of Eden.
No, I come to you like an ordinary woman
who dug up her body yesterday. I am unearthed.
Everything submerged protrudes into time.
Begin with my hip, regular motion of my pelvis
as I circulate around the rooms of my house.
This is more than a topical application of flesh.
I press against the contour of my own skin
as if it were a lover's palm. Heat is consuming.
The explanation is on the tip of my tongue.
I have eaten something besides an apple and
it made me fond of my own myriad shapes.
Once I'd have swooned before admitting I like
the motion of bodies spinning in space. Now
I'm a living embrace of planetary urges.
No, I am an ordinary woman with appetites.

Panacea

I have eaten from the tree.
I have eaten from the vine.
I have eaten from the bush.

I have put blossoms in my mouth.

And I have lain on the grasses
and looked at the sky
light coming through a single leaf
framed by my fingers.

The veins have given me direction
the wooly sheaths warmth
the spines a necessary jab.

Let the good days steep.

If you find me curled fetal
take a serrate leaf and saw me in half.
I am a magician's assistant.
I am transformed

    or merely enamored

        or hopeful.

Here is abundance.

    If I crawl under that shrub
    I will find a coin from last century.

    If I crawl under that shrub
    I will know thorns and dirt and birds scattering.

    If I crawl under that shrub
    you will know where to find me.

Because these are lost times
and I've found something anyway—

    the smallest recuperation

as if I have learned to draw water up
from the depths of the earth
or cull solace from sunlight

when really I have only taken pleasure
where offered

taken heart as a shape that occurs
naturally

taken one season by the hours
and shook down petals.

        What fruit.
        Drupe and berry.

I wanted someone to turn to.
I wanted something to turn to.
I wanted an answer.
One answer.

But the bark peels horizontally
and the bark sheds vertically
and there is no bark
only a blue-green stem of grass
hanging from my lover's lips.

Whistle.

There will be days to wrack my head
and there will be other days.

Plain days.
Sun comes up and sun goes down days.
Days held up by small green bracts.

Picture perfect.

What if I told you that today
I trust the tendrils
to hook onto time and pull me
into tomorrow?

Why I should have faith now
I don't know.

I turned my head.
I turned on my heels
and went back to see
a speck of a fleck of red
I almost walked right by.

Sometimes I don't miss everything.

Here's a paintbrush.
Whole leaf.
Broad strokes.

Cochineal on the prickly pear.
Apricot on the branch.
Moon in the sky.

Vision ripens slowly.

The bulb underground
may well rise up.
Give it a chance.

Chance something.

> Plant another crop
> for the rabbits
> for the insects
> for the hail
> for the knowledge of power
> and powerlessness.

For occasional gratitude.

For more than that, walk.

(Oh how I would like to keep my legs
and the memory of what I've done with them
intact.)

> Pine.
> The piñons are dying.
> Disease doesn't take anything for granted.

I'm learning—
my arms around a bushel of seeds
the wind in my hair.

Or my arms around the wind
and seeds everywhere.

Such prospects
and I don't have to do anything
except dwell here.

Here,
where anything can happen.

Notes on Plants

30   Achillea millefolium | Yarrow

Yarrow, also known as milfoil, thousand seal, and soldier's woundwort, derived
its scientific name from Achilles who supposedly used the plant to treat the
wounded during the Trojan War. Aside from its capacity to stop internal and
external bleeding, the plant will induce a sweat, thus releasing toxins. It is also
a uterine stimulant. I used this common plant with its bunches of white flowers
and feathery leaves to look for my own Achilles' heel. More than any physical
vulnerability, what bothered me was the fact that I'd never taken the time to
identify yarrow before beginning the series. I wanted to feel the regret, so that I
could learn to cultivate better attention.

31   Agave parryi | Century Plant

The agave's giant blossoms, which spring up suddenly on a tall pole of a stalk,
seem ripe for toppling, to my jaded eye. And, it's true that the spectacular
flowering of the century plant marks the end of this succulent perennial's long
lifespan. It lives for up to three decades, a metaphorical century. Agaves are the
source of tequila, pulque, and mescal. The fibers can also be used to make
hammocks and the sap soothes and protects both internal and external
wounds.

32   Aloe barbadensis | Aloe

Aloe has long been recognized as a wound healer, with an early reference
in the papyrus ebers, an Egyptian document dating to 1550 B.C. It is also
referenced in five places in the Bible including a beautiful passage in Numbers
24:5-6. "How lovely are your tents, O Jacob! Your dwellings, O Israel! Like valleys
that stretch out, like gardens by the riverside, like aloes planted by the Lord,
like cedars besides the water." Aloe can also be taken internally as a laxative.
I was drawn to the fact that something so soothing first requires the use of a
knife to gain access to the bounty.

33 Amaranthus hypochondriacus | Love-Lies-Bleeding

What names! Love-Lies-Bleeding couldn't be more saddled. The scientific name
comes from the Greek meaning "unwithering." The sturdy annual with crimson
tufts of flowers is an astringent that can be used to reduce heavy menstrual
flow. I wrote an astringent conversation, period.

34 Angelica archangelica | Angelica

Torn between a prayer and a tactile impulse to connect with the earth, I
turned to angelica where I could have both. Angelica, which looks sort of like

a giant 10-foot carrot, usually blooms around the feast day of St. Michael, the great defender who, in some tales, guards over the bodies of Moses and Eve to protect us from the sin of hero worship. A rich source of B12, folic acid, and niacin, angelica helps build blood cells and increase energy. It also treats indigestion and helps normalize female reproductive systems.

35 Arnica montana | **Arnica**

Also called telegraphweed and leopard's bane, source after source reported that Goethe drank arnica tea to ease his angina. If at first I found the celebrity gossip rather intrusive, ultimately it became a source of solace. Multiple sclerosis lesions present as spots on an MRI. Spots are the first thing I think of when I think of a leopard. Leopard's bane however doesn't have spots, the daisy-like flowers have yellow petals around a yellow center, more soothing than the implication. A homeopathic remedy for shock, arnica is rarely used anymore to treat the heart because of toxicity risks, but it is often employed externally to improve circulation and speed healing.

36 Artemisia frigida | **Wormwood**

I found this wormwood (also known as fringed sagebrush or little sage) in the Sandia Mountains on a day I was testing my legs. It took a while, months, after the big flare to recover any hiking abilities. I was drawn to this gray-green plant with downturned yellow flowers as a kind of kin, a mirror of sorts. Looking down at plants is far preferable to metaphorically looking down. And even "bitters" have a place in the spectrum of things. Not quite as strong as some of the other wormwoods, this plant still aids digestion, acts as a diuretic and antibiotic, as well as helping to expel worms.

37 Betula alba | **White Birch**

The pale, papery bark of white birch makes me think of the blank slate or unarticulated love letters, even the potential of life free from fate. Infusions of the leaves help remove waste products from the urine, thereby treating kidney stones or gout, the various ways we harden.

38 Calendula officinalis | **Marigold**

One of the great wound healers with extensive use in the Civil War, pot marigold staunches blood flow and works as an antiseptic preventing infection and encouraging healing. It also gets used extensively in ritual adornment throughout cultures, including Day of the Dead celebrations, partially because the brilliantly colored blossoms are able to bloom across the calendar. Eaten up visually, the bright petals also get thrown into stews and other dishes and petals can be tossed into bathwater to simply enliven bathing and soften skin. My boyfriend did give me calendula, but he knew I was writing about it.

39 Calluna vulgaris | **Heather**

A cleansing herb found around heaths and bogs, heather can be used to treat a variety of conditions ranging from kidney complaints and urinary tract infections to arthritis and muscle pain. I know the flowering shrub from time spent in Europe. I know it fondly, picture purple slopes. To learn that the greens could be used to make mattresses and the pipe-like roots to make musical instruments, just made it more endearing. Even writing the poem was like an afternoon off reminiscing.

40 Capsicum annum | **Cayenne**

Cayenne is red hot, a flared temper, a spicy meal, a passion. Heat moves things that are on the verge of getting stagnant. When rubbed on the skin, the heat of cayenne can help block other pain by overwhelming nerve signals and by neutralizing a chemical involved in the inflammatory process. It also, naturally, promotes sweating and serves as a nerve tonic.

41 Centella asiatica | **Gotu Kola**

I was so happy when I found out that gotu kola has been used to treat leprosy. I'd been feeling alienated, profoundly, and was desperate to connect with some plant that could assuage or resonate with my mood. A creeping plant with fan-shaped leaves, gotu kola gained an association with longevity because it is a preferred food of elephants. Great for skin ailments, it is also thought to help improve memory and mind function, and is being looked at for Alzheimer's disease and some childhood learning difficulties.

42 Cnicus benedictus | **Blessed Thistle**

Blessed thistle is the literal target of myth. Legend holds that when Charlemagne's men were taken ill with plague, an angel came to him in a dream and told him to shoot an arrow into the sky, and where it landed he would find the cure. The arrow struck thistle and purportedly saved his troops. Consequently, thistle, which is an antibiotic and antimicrobial, gets mentioned as a treatment against all kinds of epidemics.

43 Crataegus oxyacantha | **Hawthorn**

Hawthorn is a member of the rose family, a deciduous thorny shrub with berries and white flowers that is often cultivated into hedges. A cardiac tonic, it also increases peripheral circulation. I flashed back to my hedged-in girlhood in Europe.

44 Datura stramonium | **Jimsonweed**

Jimsonweed is poisonous. A powerful plant, people have used (and misused) it to produce a "high," an endeavor that often goes awry and leads to tremendous difficulties (or death). When I read the symptoms, I felt like I was reading about a severe MS flare, with loss of equilibrium, mobility and vision changes, not to mention confusion and "emotional lability." I feel closer to datura than I'd prefer, but having an external growing representation of my personal struggle is encouraging somehow, a patron plant.

45 Echinacea angustifolia | **Echinacea**

Since multiple sclerosis is an autoimmune disease, I can't take echinacea. The normally beneficial spike in the immune system could too readily trigger a flare. Fear is a natural response to a flare or any threat. For people with normal immune systems, echinacea can allay fear. To learn that the name came from the flower's resemblance to a hedgehog further heightened my desire to explore the way we guard ourselves. It was, rather unpleasantly, timely.

46 Fallugia paradoxa | **Apache Plume**

Apache plume gets used in landscaping all around, practically flamboyant, but I first noticed the shrub in the wild, where I found a comparatively small spread. The "paradox" of flowers and pink feathering seeds at the same time was perfectly striking. I was pleased to learn that it helps prevent erosion. In New Mexico, that matters. The root can be used to treat coughs or applied topically for joint pain and the petals work like an antacid.

47 Filipendula ulmaria | **Meadowsweet**

Near streams and ditchbanks, meadowsweet can grow to six feet tall with creamy yellow flowers and almond-scented leaves. A source of salicylic acid (now synthesized as "aspirin"), the plant is a good anti-inflammatory and pain reliever with added benefits for the heart. The name "meadowsweet" puts me into a revery of reminiscing.

48 Ginkgo biloba | **Ginkgo**

Used for loss of memory, several ginkgo trees survived the blast at Hiroshima. I worry about our culture's memory as much as the lesions in my own head knocking out details of yesterday. The tree has been referred to as the grandfather grandson tree because of its longevity. The fan-shaped leaf with a partial split down the center has even been written about by Rilke.

50 Glycyrrhiza glabra | **Licorice**

How could you not associate licorice with longing? Moreover, the root was supposedly found in King Tut's tomb. Even the simple wait time of four years before the harvest was enough for me to think of everything unrequited. A member of the pea family, this tall purple-flowered shrub has great anti-inflammatory properties, especially for the gastrointestinal system and ulcers. Licorice also has the peculiar ability to strengthen the effectiveness of other herbs and, because it can be up to fifty times sweeter than sugar, the taste can mask less palatable flavors. Licorice root is still often used to flavor tobacco.

51 Grindelia aphanactis | **Gumweed**

My boyfriend tries to convert everyone he meets to chewing the sticky yellow gumball-like flowers of gumweed. I love the shape and form and even the texture in my mouth, but am less fond of the taste. The flowers are an expectorant and antispasmodic used to treat bronchitis and coughs. They can also relieve kidney complaints, serve as a mild heart tonic, and be mashed into yet another great wound healer.

52 Gutierrezia sarothrae | **Snakeweed**

I remain intrigued by references to "disturbed" places and the plants that thrive there. The area where I walk every day is ranchland with a huge bright population of snakeweed. I take all kinds of solace out there. Snakeweed tea is used as a cleansing emetic, to reduce urinary retention, and increase strength or treat rheumatism.

53 Hamamelis virginiana | **Witch Hazel**

The "witch" in witch hazel comes from the Old English "wych," meaning any pliable branch. The branches can be used either to make brooms or as dowsing rods. I'd prefer to dowse but suspect sweeping is just as important in the scope of human affairs. High in tannins and flavonoids, the plant makes a good external astringent, soothing skin irritations and hemorrhoids. Internally it can ease diarrhea. It is astonishing in its form, with distinctive yellow flowers and seed pods that mature and manually eject the seeds tremendous distances.

54 Hydrastis canadensis | **Goldenseal**

There's a longstanding myth around goldenseal related to drug testing, which presumes that ingesting the plant can erase chemical abuses, most recently THC from urine tests. It is a myth, but even the rumor of a clean slate is alluring. Its misuse has led to overharvesting the wild crop, and concerns about fair trade. Goldenseal (the roots, not the berries) actually just works great against all kinds of infections, including ear infections. As far as I know, it has no direct benefit for the heart. The heart just got into the poem because it is always immediate and I needed a current sign.

55 Hypericum perforatum | **St. John's Wort**

Myth holds that if you place a sprig of Saint John's wort under your pillow on June 24th, St. John will appear in a dream. My interest was in the plant, so I reversed the structure. Also called goatweed and warrior's wounds, it is best known as an antidepressant, though it is also a nervous system tonic and a wound healer dating back to the Crusades. Tiny black dots on the yellow petals ooze red when crushed.

56 Juniperus monosperma | **One-Seed Juniper**

After writing the first draft of "One-Seed Juniper," I woke up from a nightmare with the profound knowledge that I didn't want to live alone anymore. I wasn't thinking about my housing set-up, rather about the way I choose to pass through the world. Juniper is a comfort plant for me and part of comfort at this stage of my life is other people. Juniper also helps balance the body, purifying and cleansing the urinary tract, treating cystitis and diarrhea, eczema and psoriasis. The berries take up to three years to ripen and provide the distinctive taste of gin.

57 Lavandula officinalis | **Lavender**

Lavender is a strewing herb used to freshen the air. It also is used in many creams and massage oils. The perennial shrub, with its spikes of violet flowers, relieves headaches and depression, and promotes restful sleep. Soothing and calming, it also has a history of use in embalming. A good plant for grieving.

58 Lobelia inflata | **Lobelia**

Lobelia is a striking plant, truthfully enough to make you gasp, that gets used to treat shortness of breath and asthma. I was interested in the dual meaning of *breathless*. Also known as pukeweed, it works as an emetic. I was hoping it would purge complacency.

59 Marrubium vulgare | **Horehound**

I found horehound on a wildflower walk by the highway. The juxtaposition of the fast-passing cars and our bent and stooped and analyzing postures got to me. Horehound's white flowers evolve into burrs containing seeds. It has downy, gray leaves and a woody, square stem. An expectorant and bitter herb, it has long been a remedy for chest complaints. It can also be used to treat liver and gallbladder complaints, improve appetite, and treat intestinal worms.

60 Matricaria recutita | **Chamomile**

Chamomile is a resilient, often underestimated plant. In *Henry IV*, Shakespeare wrote, "for though the chamomile the more it is trodden on, the faster it grows, yet youth the more it is wasted, the sooner it wears." Springing back is an ability to cherish. Also known as ground apple for its scent, Chamomile has feathery leaves and flowers that resemble a daisy— white petals and yellow centers. The botanical name *Matricaria* is derived from the Latin for "womb" because of the plant's uses for female conditions such as menstrual cramps. A muscle relaxant and sedative with antiseptic and anti-inflammatory properties, it also aids in digestion.

61 Medicago sativa | **Alfalfa**

My last book was practically set in an alfalfa field. Here I simply wanted to pay pure homage. If alfalfa is also known as *purple medics*, I created the phrase *green convalescence* to more closely capture both the nutritive value as well as the kind of greening of the green, joyous spirit of Hildegard of Bingen. "Alfalfa" comes from the Arabic meaning "father of all foods." A member of the legume family, the deep root systems are able to pull nutrients from twenty feet below the soil, making it great for any kind of recovery. It stimulates appetite and helps with nutrient assimilation.

62 Melissa officinalis | **Lemon Balm**

Lemon balm is a tall perennial with tiny white flowers and a refreshing scent. Bees like the plant, and the name *Melissa* comes from the Greek word for honey bee. It can treat digestive and sleep problems as well as depression and a variety of viruses. Since Gerard wrote that the herb "comforteth the hart and driveth away all sadnesse," I turned to it when I was feeling down despite the freshest sky.

63 Mentha piperita | **Peppermint**

Everybody knows peppermint. I wanted to write about the mood I was in that more closely resembled the pre-herb state. It helped that the square-stemmed perennial was once used to treat dog bites and wasp stings, supposedly repels rats and mice, and that it induces belching and works for headaches.

64 Oenothera biennis | **Evening Primrose**

Evening primrose oil is one of the supplements I take for MS. Also known as sundrop, king's cureall, and *yerba del golpe* (herb for bruises), evening primrose is a biennial producing only leaves the first year, flowers and seeds the second. The seeds provide essential fatty acids. Along with myriad other uses for burns, coughs, and digestion, the plant is developing a reputation with autoimmune disorders, including Sjogren's, scleroderma, MS, and rheumatoid arthritis. I think that adjusting to any chronic, life-changing diagnosis commonly takes getting into that second year to discover any fruit, acceptance as a biennial.

65 Passiflora incarnata | **Passionflower**

With the name referencing the Passion of Christ, the time between the Last Supper and the Crucifixion, I knew this poem had to be difficult and beautiful. The sheer comedy of the word "maypop" was also irresistible. Passionflower is a perennial vine with purple flowers overburdened with religious symbolism— petals as twelve apostles, three stamens as Christ's wounds, corona as crown of thorns. A tranquilizer, passionflower works well for the overactive mind, insomnia, and stress. It has also been used to treat epilepsy and neuralgia, as well as menopausal symptoms.

66 Piper methysticum | **Kava**

Kava is an alterative, with fascinating rituals surrounding its use in the Pacific Islands. Bare-breasted virgins in grass skirts would grind it in their mouths and spit it into the bowl. Or, even the mortar and pestle would be sexualized, with the bowl for grinding called "breast." Part of the pepper family with large heart-shaped leaves, the rootstock contains psychoactive substances. Cold water in-fusions release the soporific and narcotic effects, mild euphoria and tranquility.

67 Rhamnus purshianus | **Cascara Sagrada**

I was looking forward to writing "the laxative poem," saved it for the end of the series, thinking that I'd be able to get everything out of my system for the book. It took fewer words than I expected. The bark of cascara sagrada has to be stored for at least a year to reduce the violence of the purge and lose the emetic properties. A cathartic and laxative, it also increases the secretion of bile.

68 Ruta graveolens | **Rue**

Rue can be used to help induce abortions, so I was thinking about things I don't want, and grief. It turned out to be the perfect plant for the conflicted emotions of a two-bird day. I often catch towhees in my house, and occasionally the misguided mockingbird or bereft hummer. It's always traumatic trying to corner them in the window and grab them, but to have two birds two feet apart separated by a pane of glass was almost more than I could bear. An evergreen bush with small yellow flowers, rue can induce menstruation and improve eyesight, as well as treat MS and Bell's palsy. The name comes from the Greek *rua* meaning to set free.

69 Scutellaria lateriflora | **Skullcap**

Scullcap soothes nervous tension and excitability, even PMS symptoms, reducing the muscular tension associated with stress. Also known as hoodwort and madweed, at one time skullcap was credited with treating rabies, though now it's assumed that it treated the associated hydrophobia. The actual structure of the plant provides a perspective on life with flowers on one side and nothing on the other. Without ingesting anything, I can reap the benefits and remember to see both sides of the metaphorical stem.

70 Silybum marianum | **Milk Thistle**

Milk thistle is striking as a plant, myth, and medicine. The name was derived from the white veins on the plant that were attributed to a fallen drop of the Virgin Mary's breast milk. Having friends affected by the current epidemic of Hepatitis C, this plant is important to me. It helps the liver recover from exposure to viruses or toxins. It can even be used to counteract the deadly amanita mushroom if treatment is initiated quickly enough.

71 Symphytum officinale | **Comfrey**

Tales of boiling water with comfrey and getting two distinct pieces of flesh (ie. beef and chicken) to literally stick together led to the exploration of comfrey's consider comfrey a shoe-in for marriage. After I wrote the poem, I dreamt that the institution of marriage was controlled by the mafia. I worked, rather ineptly, for the mob typing up licenses for couples on broken computers while an unused spinning wheel sat between floors of the elevator. Comfrey, a member of the borage family, is also called ass ear, boneset, knitback, and consound.

72 Tanacetum parthenium | **Feverfew**

Feverfew, also known as featherfoil and midsummer daisy, treats migraines, drives out fevers, and also relieves nervous tension. It has been used to expel roundworm and treat scabies. I'm very lucky in that the stomach-sickening headaches I get are usually a result of thinking too much (often after an unresolved argument) and I've learned that I can back off a bit emotionally and sometimes suffer a bit less. This ability to control the headaches, a bit, reminded me of feverfew's ability to reduce the amount and frequency of vomiting with migraines.

73 Taraxacum officinale | **Dandelion**

Dandelion, also known as blowball, lion's tooth, and priest's crown, is the scourge of the grass lawn and the delight of children and herbalists. A rich source of vitamins and minerals, the dandelion's bitter compounds, found in the leaves and roots, help stimulate digestion and improve fat metabolism. For months after the diagnosis, out of fear I consciously curtailed all expression of desire. I was stuck in the claustrophobic mindset of sickness where you can't plan for the future or allow yourself to hope for much of anything. The return of simple playful wants has been a blessing, and a sign that I'm accepting life with disease.

74 Thelesperma filifolium | **Cota**

Plants like cota really please me. Small, unflashy, local, in my yard. Also known as greenthread, cota is a sparse representation of "flower," offering up just a smidgen of color despite the fact that each blossom is actually a tiny cluster of yellow flowers. The tea makes a mild diuretic and antiseptic, as well as soothing indigestion, arthritis, kidney and blood complaints.

75 Ulmus fulva | **Slippery Elm**

The inner rind of slippery elm is a demulcent, strongly mucilaginous. It soothes and coats and, thus, can offer aid for external wounds, as well as for the throat and digestive system, ulcers, and irritable bowel syndrome. The elm suffered a severe setback with Dutch Elm Disease in the '60s. The tree continues to recover.

76 Urtica dioica | **Stinging Nettle**

I grew up with stinging nettles in England. I remember lining tree forts with them to stave off other kids. At the time, I also knew which plants could assuage nettle sting. Along with welts, nettles raise really interesting questions, akin to the underlying assumption of homeopathy: like curing like. The whole concept of "counter-irritant" is intriguing, and I think , often manifest in non-health realms more than we realize. Nettles stimulate circulation and cleanse the system, and also provide relief from arthritis and neuralgia, sprains, and sciatica.

77 Vaccinium myrtillus | **Bilberry**

Bilberry is fascinating. Some of the plant's medicinal value has long been recognized. Hildegard of Bingen, for example, suggested it for inducing menstruation, and other herbalists knew it for its uses in intestinal conditions, rheumatism and gout. However, World War II brought a whole new use to light. British Royal Air Force pilots reported an improvement in night vision during bombing raids after having eaten bilberry jam. This led to more research, which illuminated bilberry's effects on the eyes and vascular system. Usually war just makes use of medical discoveries, but here war led to the discovery.

78 Valeriana officinalis | **Valerian**

Valerian stinks, consequently Greek physicians Galen and Dioscorides dubbed the plant "phu." It has also been referred to as the herb of cats since they are attracted to the stench of the drying root, and legend links valerian to the allure of the Pied Piper. It gets its name from the Latin verb for "to be happy," since it treats nervousness, anxiety, and sleep disorders. It also soothes muscle cramps and restless leg syndrome. Moreover, it has a long history around war times. It was actually distributed during WWII in England to help people remain calm and get some sleep during air raids.

79 Verbascum thapsus | **Mullein**

Also known as torchweed, flannelflower, and hedge taper, mullein's tall stems, which can be up to six feet, used to be burned in funeral processions. It treats dry coughs and throat inflammations, but on the day I needed mullein, what got to me was the pure ascending shape and the striking contrast between the first-year and the second-year growth. I thought, here is as good an opportunity as any to underestimate potential.

80 Vitex agnus-castus | **Chaste Tree**

Chaste tree, also known as monk's pepper, developed a reputation for being able to curb sexual desire. Even though there is no clinical evidence to support this use, the branches and flowers have been employed in countless rituals throughout history, including having the blossoms strewn as novitiates took vows to enter monasteries. Related to the grape, chaste tree has purple blossoms and red-black berries that can be used to treat female hormonal problems, including PMS, irregular menstrual cycles, and ironically, infertility.

81 Yucca glauca | **Yucca**

When I first moved to New Mexico, I was immediately drawn to yucca with its gaping maw of a seedpod emerging from spikes of green. I spent months, literally, sketching it. Now that I've acclimated to the desert, I'm no less struck by yuccas, only now I find the greatest startle when I see the furry exposed roots. In coyote country, my first thought is always inevitably, "Oh, another kill"— because I find things like fox legs and rabbit torsos, whole skeletons of downed cows. No matter what I register intellectually, I can't quite escape that visceral reaction. Yucca breaks down waste in the body, improves intestinal flora, is an anti-inflammatory which can help regenerate connective tissue, as well as fight the early stages of certain cancers. The root can also be used to make soap and provide the foam of root beer.

82 Zingiber officinale | **Ginger**

Although ginger is often thought to resemble a hand or thumb, the root reminds me more of the female form, the early earth mother statues and fertility symbols. It has been mentioned by Marco Polo, Confucius, and appears in the Koran. Medieval Europe thought it came from the Garden of Eden. It treats all kinds of nausea, including motion sickness, and also promotes sweating, warms and soothes the body. It has many other uses, including treating Raynaud's disease, improving circulation, and treating heart disease, strokes, and chronic fatigue.

Selected bibliography and suggested readings

"American Botanical Council Herbal Gram." 2006. http://www.herbalgram.org/herbalgram/ (February 21, 2006).

Brill, "Wildman" Steve, and Evelyn Dean. *Identifying and Harvesting Edible and Medicinal Plants in Wild (and Not So Wild) Places.* New York: Quill, A Harper Resource Book, 1994.

Carter, Jack L., Martha A. Carter, and Donna J. Stevens. *Common Southwestern Native Plants: An Identification Guide.* Silver City, NM: Mimbres Publishing, 2003.

Dunmire, William W., and Gail D. Tierney. *Wild Plants of the Pueblo Province: Exploring Ancient and Enduring Uses.* Santa Fe, NM: Museum of New Mexico Press, 1995.

Foster, Steven. "Steven Foster Group Herbal Information Resources." 2006. http://www.stevenfoster.com/education/index.html (February 21, 2006).

Foster, Steven and Christopher Hobbs. *A Field Guide to Medicinal Plants.* New York: Houghton Mifflin, 2002.

"Henriette's Herbal Homepage." 2006. http://www.henriettesherbal.com/ (February 21, 2006).

"Herbal Information Center and Vitamin Directory." 2006. http://www.kcweb.com/herb/herbmain.htm/ (February 21, 2006).

"Herb Directory Index." 2006. http://www.holistic-online.com/Herbal-Med/Hol_Herb_Directory_Index.htm/ (February 21, 2006).

"Herbs." 2006. http://www.innvista.com/health/herbs/default.htm/ (February 21, 2 06).

Grieve, Maud. "A Modern Herbal." http://botanical.com/botanical/mgmh/comindxa.html (February 21, 2006).

Kwant, Cor. "The Gingko Pages." 2006. www.xs4all.nl/~kwanten/ (February 21, 2006).

Moore, Michael. *Medicinal Plants of the Mountain West*, Rev. and enl. ed. Santa Fe, NM: Museum of New Mexico Press, 2003.

Plyler, Sheri & Charlie. "Indian Spring Herbal Encyclopedia." 2005. www.indianspringherbs.com (February 21, 2006).

Rudgley, Richard. "Kava." *The Encyclopedia of Psychoactive Substances.* 1998. www.biopsychiatry.com/kava/ (Feruary 21, 2006).

Permissions Acknowledgments

The author wishes to thank Al Davis for all his support over the years, Stephanie Schilling, and Michelle Peterson for considerate and thorough editing of the manuscript, and everyone at New Rivers Press who has made this book possible.

Some of these poems first appeared in *Central Avenue*.

"Ginkgo Biloba" appears in the 2006 Nuclear Resistance Calendar published by the Albuquerque Peace Center.

"Potentilla Tormentilla" is recorded on *Albuzerxque* #13   (Zerx 050)

A large number of these poems are recorded as duets with trombonist Kurt Heyl on a CD, also titled *Mortar & Pestle*.

About the author

Lisa Gill was born in Minot, North Dakota, and now makes her home in Moriarty, New Mexico, with two dogs and a cat. Her poems have appeared in numerous publications including *Blue Collar Review, Desperado, Prosodia, Red Weather, The Weekly Alibi*, as well as *The Harwood Anthology* and *In Company: An Anthology of New Mexican Poets after 1960*. One of her short stories, "Holding Zeno's Suitcase in Kansas, Flowering," won first prize in the 7th volume of *American Fiction: The Best Unpublished Short Stories by Emerging Writers*, and was nominated for a Pushcart Prize. She frequently works with artists and musicians, and has performed widely, from the Seattle Poetry Festival to the Taos Poetry Circus and the Thom McGrath Visiting Writers Series in Moorhead, Minnesota. Her first poetry collection, *Red as a Lotus: Letters to a Dead Trappist*, one hundred poems dedicated to Thomas Merton, was published with La Alameda Press in 2002. She recently premiered *Caput Nili*, a one-woman show addressing violence at Out Ch'Yonda in Albuquerque, New Mexico. *Mortar & Pestle* is her second book.